A
WITTGENSTEIN
WORKBOOK

by

Members of the Department of Philosophy
The University of Leeds

Christopher Coope   *Timothy Potts*
Peter Geach   *Roger White*

UNIVERSITY OF CALIFORNIA PRESS
Berkeley and Los Angeles

UNIVERSITY OF CALIFORNIA PRESS

Berkeley and Los Angeles, California

ISBN 0-520-01840-0

Library of Congress Catalog Card No.: 79-135161

Manufactured in the United States of America

Contents

Preface

The material in this booklet has been used to introduce undergraduates in their final year to the philosophy of Wittgenstein. This has proved a difficult task; Wittgenstein frequently approaches questions in philosophy from such a radically original standpoint that people are bewildered by what he has to say and lack the basic orientation of thought to appreciate the force of his remarks. Overlooking his hard philosophical arguments, people come to regard the *Tratatus* as an arcane curiosity in the history of philosophy and the *Investigations* as a series of platitudes, and accordingly dismiss Wittgenstein's writings as something that a serious student of philosophy can with impunity ignore. For lack of this basic orientation, they have approached him expecting answers to the questions which were not his questions and have thereby overlooked the questions which he does raise and attempts to answer. Thus Carnap and others have seen in the *Tractatus* an attempt to supply prescriptions for an ideal language, whereas Wittgenstein from first to last was concerned to show how language as it is actually works.

There is a prevalent impression that Wittgenstein's later philosophy involved rejection of all or most of the doctrines of the *Tractatus*. To correct this, we have devised a programme of topics emphasizing those which are taken up in both the *Tractatus* and the *Investigations*, to the end that the changes in Wittgenstein's views may be set within a framework which shows the continuity of his thought (cp. his wish, expressed in his introduction to the *Investigations*, that the *Tractatus* and it might be published together in a single volume). In choosing these topics we were greatly assisted by Professor G. E. M. Anscombe, who also helped in compiling the references and readings.

The programme was prepared for use in seminars and it seemed natural in the circumstances to experiment with a set of questions designed both to show the student what kinds of question he ought to be asking himself while reading the texts and also to provide material for group discussion. Hence what we offer in these pages is an aid to the interpretation of Wittgenstein's thought, not an interpretation: we aim to help the reader to interpret the texts for himself. There are in fact several strong disagreements between us on important points of interpretation; at the same time it will be apparent that we have worked from certain shared beliefs. In addition to the point already made about the continuity of Wittgenstein's thought, we may specify: that the most important single influence on Wittgenstein was Frege, and that this is true of the late as well as of the early work, where the influence is so much closer to the surface; that the connexions between Wittgenstein's philosophy and other philosophies which go under the name of 'linguistic' or 'ordinary language' philosophy, such as the writings of Austin and his followers, rarely amount to more than surface similarities; and that Wittgenstein was constantly concerned to bring out logical differences (which, as he once said, are always *big* differences) rather than idiomatic niceties. We regard these beliefs as controversial only in that they have been controverted.

We have usually tried in each question-sheet to relate the individual points into a coherent theme so as to make possible a progressive discussion in which the attempt to answer each question leads naturally to its successor, and in which from easier questions one advances gradually to more difficult ones. There are three sorts of question; those at the beginning are more straight-forward questions of interpretation, where we are relatively confident that there is an unequivocal answer which an alert student should be able to formulate; then there are questions which raise the problems central to the topic; and finally, some questions which although less central may provoke students to further thought.

The basic texts used in the programme are the *Tractatus* and the *Investigations*; the earlier topics give prominence to the former, the later topics to the latter, but cross-references to relevant passages in the other work are given wherever possible. We have also drawn on the other published works of Wittgenstein (except *Philosophische Grammatik*, which appeared too recently) in an ancillary role, since they often provide substantial aid in understanding compressed or particularly difficult passages in the two main works. The *Notebooks* play this role in relation to the *Tractatus*, the *Blue and Brown Books* and *Zettel* in relation to the *Investigations*, while the *Philosophische Bemerkungen* provides an important link between the two main works. Occasional references have been made to *Remarks on the Foundations of Mathematics*, but for the most part we have avoided involvement in questions in the philosophy of mathematics. We have had to draw heavily on Wittgenstein's last work, *On Certainty*, for topic 9, because it contains Wittgenstein's most explicit discussion of scepticism. Obviously nobody can hope to profit by our references to Wittgenstein's texts unless he treats each book Wittgenstein wrote, not just as a source-book for discussion of a particular topic, but as a coherent book in its own right. We have had to exercise our judgment in drawing up a limited but useful list of references for each topic.

Similarly, our lists of relevant secondary material make no claim to be exhaustive; we have merely detailed some writings that struck us, in very different ways, as valuable. We have made occasional explicit references to Frege but no attempt at systematic cross-reference, because the connexions between his work and Wittgenstein's are too numerous; we hold that a student who is really to come to grips with Wittgenstein's thought should carefully study 'the great works of Frege' as wholes. An appendix gives a series of cross-references to Russell's *Principles of Mathematics*; it is clear that the unresolved problems of this work were more significant for Wittgenstein than the solutions offered in *Principia Mathematica*. We include in particular cross-reference to the appendix in *Principles* on Frege, since Wittgenstein clearly read Frege partly through Russell's eyes. A second appendix lists cross-references between William James's *Principles of Psychology* and Wittgenstein's later work; Wittgenstein regarded James as a classical exponent of the tradition in the philosophy of mind that he was opposing, and James's views are often alluded to, when he is not mentioned by name, in the *Investigations* and the *Zettel*. Other authors have been cited under the heading of 'Readings' in each opening, as we judged best for the given topic.

Our experience has shown that seminars based on the discussion of the questions here presented led to more effective participation than the traditional method of discussing a student's paper. We have therefore decided to expose our teaching method to the criticism of a wider public, and should be glad of any suggestions for improving this work-book.

CHRISTOPHER COOPE
PETER GEACH
TIMOTHY POTTS
ROGER WHITE

Department of Philosophy
The University of Leeds
Leeds   LS2 9JT
June 1970

Abbreviations
used in giving references

WORKS BY WITTGENSTEIN:

N: *Notebooks 1914–1916;* Oxford, Basil Blackwell, 1961. Followed by page number.

T: *Tractatus Logico-Philosophicus;* London: Routledge and Kegan Paul, 1922 (Ogden and Richards translation); 1961 (Pears and McGuinness translation). Followed by sentence number.

PB: *Philosophische Bemerkungen;* Oxford: Basil Blackwell, 1964. Followed by section and paragraph numbers.

BlB: The Blue Book, in *The Blue and Brown Books;* Oxford: Basil Blackwell, 1958. Followed by page number.

BrB: The Brown Book, in *The Blue and Brown Books.* Followed by section and paragraph numbers.

I: *Philosophical Investigations;* Oxford: Basil Blackwell, 1953. Part I: followed by 1.*n*, where *n* is the paragraph number. Part II: followed by 2.*n*, where *n* is the section number, and then by the page number in brackets.

RFM: *Remarks on the Foundations of Mathematics;* Oxford: Basil Blackwell, 1956. Followed by section (appendix) and paragraph numbers.

Z: *Zettel;* Oxford: Basil Blackwell, 1967. Followed by paragraph number.

C: *On Certainty;* Oxford: Basil Blackwell, 1969. Followed by paragraph number.

WORKS BY FREGE (references are to page numbers):

F(GB):   *Translations from the Philosophical Writings of Gottlob Frege*, edited by Peter Geach and Max Black; Oxford: Basil Blackwell, 1960 (second edition).

FA: *The Foundations of Arithmetic :* A logico-mathematical enquiry into the concept of Number. English translation by J. L. Austin. Oxford: Basil Blackwell, 1953 (second edition).

FB: *Begriffsschrift;* in Jean van Heijenoort, *From Frege to Gödel;* Cambridge: Harvard University Press, 1967; pp. 1–82.

FG: *Grundgesetze der Arithmetik;* Jena, 1893 (photographic reprint: Hildesheim: Georg Olms, 1962). Part translated in F(GB) and part in

FG(F): *The Basic Laws of Arithemetic:* Exposition of the System; translated and edited, with an introduction, by Montgomery Furth; Berkeley and Los Angeles: University of California Press, 1964.

OTHER WORKS:

RPM: Bertrand Russell, *The Principles of Mathematics;* London: Allen and Unwin, 1937 (second edition). Followed by paragraph number.

JPP: William James, *The Principles of Psychology;* London: Macmillan, 1910. Followed by volume and page number.

AT: G. E. M. Anscombe, *An Introduction to Wittgenstein's Tractatus;* London: Hutchinson University Library, 1967 (third edition). Followed by page number.

1

THE PICTURE-THEORY

TEXTS:

N: 5–9
T: 1–3.144
PB: 10, 20, 21, 34, 67, 68, 70
I: 1. 139–141, 518–524; 2. iv, ix (p.187)
Z: 239–253, 290–292

READINGS:

1 Leibniz, *Dialogue on the Connection between Things and Words;* in *Leibniz: Selections*, edited by Philip P. Wiener; New York: Charles Scribner's Sons, 1951; 6–11

2 Hertz, *Principles of Mechanics presented in a new form;* London, Macmillan, 1899 (reprinted as Dover p/b); Author's Preface; Introduction; Dynamical Models, 175–177

3 Russell, *The Philosophy of Logical Atomism;* in *Logic and Knowledge;* London: Allen and Unwin, 1956; 177–343

4 AT: 64–71

5 N. Goodman, *Languages of Art: An Approach to a Theory of Symbols;* London: Oxford University Press, 1969

6 N. Malcolm, article on Wittgenstein in *The Encyclopaedia of Philosophy*

THE PICTURE-THEORY

QUESTIONS:

1 Explain the difference between 'depict' (*abbilden*) and 'represent' (*darstellen*) in the *Tractatus*, also the difference between these and 'go proxy for' (*vertreten*).

2 'There must be something identical in a picture and what it depicts, to enable the one to be a picture of the other at all' (T:2.161). Elucidate.

3 'It is obvious that a proposition of the form "aRb" strikes us as a picture' (T:4.012). *How* does it strike us as a picture?

4 Must a picture consist of elements in relation representing things in an analogous relation?

5 Can a picture have a negation which is also a picture? (N:33, last paragraph; I:p.11, note).

6 What is the force of saying that a picture is a fact (T:2.141)?

7 On Wittgenstein's account of picturing, why isn't the world a picture of language?

8 'Every picture is also a logical picture' (T:2.182). Explain.

9 Is the picture below a picture of an impossible state of affairs?

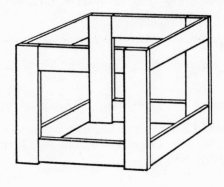

2

NAMING

READINGS:

1 Frege, FA: x, 67–72 (especially 71)

2 Russell, *Introduction to Mathematical Philosophy*; London: Allen and Unwin, 1919; chapters 16 and 17

3 M. A. E. Dummett, 'Nominalism'
   (a) in *The Philosophical Review* 65 (1956), 491–505
   (b) in *Essays on Frege*, edited by E. D. Klemke; Urbana: University of Illinois Press, 1968; 321–336

4 John R. Searle, 'Proper Names'
   (a) in *Mind* 67 (1958), 166–173
   (b) in *Philosophical Logic*, edited by P. F. Strawson; London: Oxford University Press, 1967; 89–96

5 AT: 13, 17–18, 41–50

6 W. V. Quine, *Word and Object*; Cambridge: The M.I.T. Press, 1960; sections 37–38

7 P. T. Geach, 'Naming and Predicating'; in *Essays on Frege*; 349–375

8 H. Ishiguro, 'Use and Reference of Names'; in *Studies in the Philosophy of Wittgenstein*, edited by Peter Winch; London: Routledge and Kegan Paul, 1969; 20–50

QUESTIONS

1 Is the meaning of a name the object for which it stands? (T:3.203; RPM: 46, 51, 99; I:1.40).

2 Does a name go proxy for its bearer? (T:3.22).

3 'Names *cannot* be anatomized by means of definitions' (T:3.261). Why?

4 'We may say, following Russell: the name "Moses" can be defined by means of various descriptions . . .' (I:1.79). Can it?

5 'Only in the context of a proposition does a name refer' (T:3.3, after FA:x). What is the force of this doctrine? (cf.T:3.261, last sentence; PB: 12–14; I:1.49; F(GB):32).

6 Are names the only *primitive* signs in the *Tractatus*? (T:5.472).

7 Can there be a proposition which consists only of names in concatenation? (T:4.22–4.221; 3.141–3.142; F(GB):54–55; RPM:54; AT:102,108–111).

8 Can relations be named? (T:3.1432–3.144; cf.N:14,61; F(GB):54–55; RPM:49).

9 Does the *Tractatus* envisage the possibility of a language containing no proper names? (T:5.526). If so, how does this relate to the rest of the *Tractatus*? (cf. Readings 6 and 8).

10 'In the *Tractatus*, I was unclear about logical analysis and ostensive definition. I thought then that there was "a hooking of language onto reality"' (*Wittgenstein und der Wiener Kreis*, p.209f.). What doctrines of the *Tractatus* is Wittgenstein here criticizing?

3

ANALYSIS AND COMPLEXITY

TEXTS:

N: 11(12.10.14), 46(9.5.15), 47(13.5.15)-49(20.5.15.), 59(14.6.15)-66, 69-71
(top)
T: 3.2-4.0311
PB: 1, 46, 115, 147, 205; App.1, Complex and Fact
I: 1.46-64
Z: 334-338

READINGS:

1   Plato, *Theaetetus* 201D4-202C5 (cf.I:1.46)

2   Russell, RPM: 46-55, 80-85, 133-139

3   AT: 25-40

4   N. Malcolm, 'Wittgenstein's *Philosophische Bemerkungen*'; *The Philoso-phical Review* 76(1967), 220-229

5   P. Long, 'Are Predicates and Relational Expressions Incomplete?' in *The Philosophical Review* 78(1969), 90-98

ANALYSIS AND COMPLEXITY

1 Is the *Tractatus* describing an ideal language? (T:5.5563, 4.002, 4.013, 3.323–3.325; I:1.98; contrast Russell's Preface to T (and cf. N:131)).

2 'The requirement that simple signs be possible is the requirement that sense be determinate' (T:3.23, 3.251; I:1.99–107).
(*a*) What sense or senses can be attached to the expression 'determinate sense'? (N:63–71).
(*b*) How does Wittgenstein link these two requirements?

3 Can it depend upon the truth of another proposition whether a proposition has sense? (T:2.0211).

4 Can Wittgenstein consistently with his requirements about determinateness of sense say that a proposition about a complex 'leaves something undetermined'? (T:3.24).

5 Why, according to Wittgenstein, can one not describe objects and not name situations (*Sachlagen*)? (T:3.144, 3.221).

6 Must the bearers of (logically) proper names be simple? (T:2.02, 3.203; I:1.39, 59–64).

7 Is it an objection to the *Tractatus* that Wittgenstein can give no example of a simple object? (T:5.5–5.51).

8 Are only *elementary* propositions pictures? (T:3.01,2.15).

9 'A proposition has one and only one complete analysis' (T:3.25; F(GB): 49–50; I:1.89–98). Does it make sense to talk about *the* analysis of a proposition?

10 Is there any truth in the view that what is known and understood must be complex? (I:1.46; cf. Reading 1).

11 How far does the *Tractatus* confuse complexes and facts? (cf.PB: App.I).

4

TRUTH

QUESTIONS:

1 What is the relation between a picture theory of meaning and a picture theory of truth?

2 'A picture agrees with reality or fails to agree; it is correct or incorrect, true or false.' (T:2.21; cf. I:1.429). How far can this fact about (some) pictures be used to throw light on the notion of the truth or falsity of a proposition?

3 *Must* it be possible to understand a proposition independently of understanding whether it is true or false? (T:2.22–2.225, 4.061; cf. 3.04, 3.05; I:1.433–437, 461–465).

4 Does one completely specify the sense of a proposition by specifying its truth conditions? (T:4.431, 4.463, 4.024; FG(F): 89–90).

5 Why doesn't it just happen to be so, that truth and falsity exhaust the possibilities for a proposition? (T:6.11. 4.063; I:1.447).

6 What is the law of the excluded middle? (cf. Reading 6). Could one reject the law of the excluded middle and still maintain a truth-falsity polarity for all propositions? (cf. PB:173).

7 Is a language in which 'p' says what we now say by '$\sim p$' and vice versa possible? If so, what does this possibility show? (T:4.062,5.5151).

8 Has an unasserted proposition a truth-value? (T:4.064–4.0641; I:p.11, note; RPM:52).

9 Can what the *Tractatus* calls a senseless proposition, in that it says nothing, be true or false? (T:4.46–4.4661).

5

NONSENSE VERSUS SENSELESSNESS

TEXTS:

N: 24(2.11.14), 54(3.6.15); Appendix 2(115,117,121)
T: Preface p.3; 3.24, 4.003, 4.0312–4.53, 5.473, 5.5303, 5.5351, 5.5422, 5.5571,
   6.51, 6.54; 4.461, 5.132, 5.1362
PB: 9
I:1.251–252, 344–349, 496–500, 511–514, 516–517, 520–521, 588
Z: 131–134, 255–275, 685–694

READINGS:

1 Kant, *Critique of Pure Reason*, translated by Norman Kemp Smith;
   London: Macmillan, 1933; 268–275 (for question 12)

2 Frege, 'On the Foundations of Geometry'
   (a) in *The Philosophical Review* 69 (1960),3–17
   (b) re-printed in *Essays on Frege*, 559–575

3 JPP: I.261–264

4 Hempel, 'The Empiricist Criterion of Meaning'; in *Logical Positivism*
   (edited by A. J. Ayer); Glencoe: Free Press, 1933; 108–129

5 P. F. Strawson, *Introduction to Logical Theory;* London: Methuen, 1952;
   p.3

6 AT: 150–154

7 P. Long, 'Modality and Tautology', in *Proceedings of the Aristotelian
   Society* 60 (1959–60), 27–36

8 P. T. Geach, *Mental Acts;* London: Routledge and Kegan Paul, 1960
   (second impression, corrected); p.85 (for question 5)

9 J. Bennett, 'A Myth about Logical Necessity'; *Analysis* 21 (1960–61), 59–63

10 John Passmore, *Philosophical Reasoning;* London: Gerald Duckworth,
   1961; chapter 7

NONSENSE VERSUS SENSELESSNESS

QUESTIONS:

1 Explain Wittgenstein's distinction between senselessness and nonsense.

2 Why does Wittgenstein stigmatize the propositions of mathematics as pseudo-propositions? (T:6.2–6.22; FA: 23–24).

3 ' "A knows that p is the case" is senseless if "p" is a tautology' (T:5.1362). Ought Wittgenstein to say this?

4 'There is a lack of clarity about what part *imaginability* plays in our investigation. Namely about the extent to which it ensures that a proposition makes sense' (I:1.395). How far *is* imaginability a necessary or a sufficient condition of sense? (cf. FA:x).

5 Is the fact that someone genuinely thinks he means something a guarantee that there is something that he means? (T:5.61; 5.5422; 3.031; 5.473–5.4733; Reading 8).

6 What use can you imagine for the sentence 'Seven is a number'? (T:4.126–4.1272).

7 What hangs on the question whether 'Seven is red' is nonsense or false? (T:5.4733; PB:7–8; F(GB):159–172; AT:123ff.).

8 'We cannot give a sign the wrong sense' (T:4.732). Why not?

9 'Contradicting oneself is like writing something down and then erasing it, or putting a line through it. A contradiction cancels itself and leaves nothing' (Reading 5). Then why chide a person for contradicting himself?

10 ' "Somebody" is not the name of somebody.' To what extent can we call the negation of a nonsense true? (cf. T:6.54; I:1.252 and T:4.112; AT:85).

11 Does T:6.53 follow from Wittgenstein's distinction between nonsense and senselessness?

12 Discuss the value of the ladder metaphor (T:6.54). [Can Kant's use of 'noumenon in the negative sense' be treated as showing that Kant would at times wish to regard his talk of noumena in the same light? (cf. Reading 1)] (cf. T:4.112; I:1.464; F(GB):54–55).

6

'I'
(Consciousness; *Äusserungen*)

TEXTS:

N:49, 72–73(11.6.16), 79(2.8.16), 80, 85
T:5.6–5.641
PB: 57–66, 72–73
BlB: 61–74
I: 1.398–420; 2.ix,x
Z: 65, 394–403, 535–564

READINGS:

1 Kant, *Critique of Pure Reason:* The Paralogisms of Pure Reason (Kemp
   Smith translation 328–383)

2 Schopenhauer, *The World as Will and Idea;* London: Routledge and Kegan
   Paul, 1883 (3 vols.); III.285

3 JPP: I.297–305; also, on 'ownership' of experiences, I.225–227, 331–342

4 A. N. Prior, *Papers on Time and Tense;* Oxford: at the Clarendon Press,
   1968; Ch.II On Spurious Egocentricity, 15–25

5 A. Kenny, *Descartes: A Study of his Philosophy;* New York: Random
   House, 1968; Ch. 3 and 4

6 P. T. Geach, *God and the Soul;* London: Routledge and Kegan Paul, 1969;
   6–10

6

'I'
(Consciousness; *Äusserungen*)

QUESTIONS:

1 Did Descartes give himself any grounds for believing that Descartes existed? (cf. JPP:I.273, last footnote).

2 Expound the analogy between the eye and the metaphysical subject (T:5.633 ff.).

3 Is it nonsense to say: 'I know that I am in pain'? What consequences follow?

4 If we construe I:1.244 as a possible account of how a child learns to use the sentence 'I am in pain', could an analogous account be given of how it learns 'I am not in pain'? How would the two accounts be related?

5 'what solipsism is after, is quite correct' (T:5.62). What is it after? (cf. PB:58; AT:166–168).

6 To think of the soul as a simple substance is 'to confuse the unity of experience with the experience of unity' (Kant). What is the connexion between this and T:5.62?

7 Does the supposition 'If I were you . . . ' make sense? If so, what sense? How does this compare with 'If only it were Christmas now!'?

8 If an unconscious man mutters: 'I am unconscious', is he speaking the truth? (Z:394–403).

9 'What in my experience justifies the "my" in "I feel *my* pain"? Where is the multiplicity of feeling that justifies this word? and can it only be justified when another word can step into its place?' (PB:63).

10 'Are the words "I am afraid" a description of a state of mind?' (I:2,ix — whole of section).

11 W. in an Oxford discussion: 'If a man says to me, looking at the sky, "I think it will rain, therefore I exist," I do not understand him.' Why not?

12 'That's all very fine; what we want to know is: is the *cogito* valid or not?' (Prichard in reply to Wittgenstein in the same Oxford discussion). Well, is it?

7

LOGIC AS THE MIRROR OF THE WORLD

TEXTS:

N: 107, 116
T: 4.116–4.1212, 5–6.13 (especially 5.511, 5.5563 and 6.124)
PB: 54
I: 1.89–108, 547–558 (negation), 561–568 ('is')

READINGS:

1 J. Łukasiewicz, 'W obronie Logistyki'; in *Z zagadnień logiki i filozofii*;
   Warsaw: Paustwowe Wydawnictwo Naukowe, 1961 (translated by
   Peter Geach):
   As a conclusion to these remarks, I should like to sketch a picture
   connected with the deepest intuitive feelings I always get about logistic.
   This picture perhaps throws more light than any discursive exposition
   would on the real foundations from which this science grows (at least so
   far as I am concerned). Whenever I am occupied even with the tiniest
   logistical problem, e.g. trying to find the shortest axiom of the im-
   plicational calculus, I have the impression that I am confronted with a
   mighty construction, of indescribable complexity and immeasurable
   rigidity. This construction has the effect upon me of a concrete tangible
   object, fashioned from the hardest of materials, a hundred times
   stronger than concrete and steel. I cannot change anything in it; by
   intense labour I merely find in it ever new details, and attain unshakable
   and eternal truths. Where and what is this ideal construction? A
   Catholic philosopher would say: it is in God, it is God's thought.

2 AT: 161–166

LOGIC AS THE MIRROR OF THE WORLD

QUESTIONS:

1 What is shown by a proposition's being a tautology?

2 'The logical propositions . . . presuppose that names have meaning, and that elementary propositions have sense' (T:6.124). Do the logical propositions *show* what the simple objects are? (cf. I:1.58).

3 'If we know, on purely logical grounds, that there must be elementary propositions, then this must be known by anyone who understands propositions in their unanalysed form' (T:5.5562). Is this not an objection to Wittgenstein's own theory?

4 Give some illustrations of T:3.3421.

5 'The logic of the world which the propositions of logic show in tautologies, mathematics shows in equations' (T:6.22). Discuss (a) this comparison, (b) this contrast.

6 Why is it Wittgenstein's *fundamental* thought that the 'logical constants' are not surrogates? (T:4.0312).

7 'There is only *logical* necessity' (T:6.37). What truth is there in this? (cf. AT:158–160).

8 'At the basis of the whole modern view of the world lies the illusion that the so-called laws of nature are the explanations of natural phenomena' (T:6.371). Why an illusion?

9 'Laws like the principle of sufficient reason, etc., treat of the network and not of what the network describes' (T:6.35). Do they then show anything about the world? (cf. T:6.31–6.3611; Z:677–680).

10 'But the essence of language is a picture of the essence of the world; and philosophy as trustee of grammar can actually grasp the essence of the world, only not in propositions of language, but in rules for this language which eliminate nonsensical combinations of signs' (PB:54). What does he mean by calling logic the trustee of grammar?

11 'The concept of a perspicuous representation is of fundamental significance for us. It earmarks the form of account we give, the way we look at things.' (I:1.122), Give examples of how the discovery of a more perspicuous representation has altered the way we look at things. (cf. AT:138–141).

8

SHOWING AND SAYING

TEXTS:

N: Appendix II; 44 (1.v.15)
T: Preface, 6.521–7, 4.113–4.128, 2.17–2.182, 3.262, 4.02–4.027
PB: 6, 47–56

READINGS:

1   Frege, 'On Concept and Object'; F(GB):42–55

2   M. A. E. Dummett, 'Frege on Functions: A Reply'
    (a) in *The Philosophical Review* 64 (1955), 96–107
    (b) in *Essays on Frege*, 268–283

3   M. A. E. Dummett, 'Note: Frege on Functions'
    (a) in *The Philosophical Review* 65 (1956), 229–230
    (b) in *Essays on Frege*, 295–297

8

SHOWING AND SAYING

QUESTIONS:

1 'What does not get expressed in the signs is shown by their application. What is latent in the signs is patent in their application' (T:3.262). What then shows that 'five', 'red' and 'apple' in I:1.1 are of different categories?

2 Explain Wittgenstein's distinction between formal concepts and concepts proper (T:4.126–4.1274; cf. AT:82–86, 122–131).

3 Explain the connexion between the notion of a formal concept and that of a variable (T:4.126–4.1274; 3.31–3.318; 5.501).

4 'A picture cannot however depict its pictorial from: it displays it' (T:2.172). Why is this? (cf. T:2.172–2.18; 4.121–4.1212).

5 Can we get around Wittgenstein's difficulties about saying, e.g., '7 is a number' by saying instead: ' "7" is a numeral'? (T:p.xxii; AT:82–85).

6 'The meanings of primitive signs can be explained by the illustrative use of examples. Examples are propositions which use the primitive signs, i.e. propositions which cannot be understood until one already knows the meanings of these signs' (T:3.263; PB:6). How does this connect with the showing/saying distinction?

7 Under what circumstances can pointing out that a certain string of words is nonsensical show something philosophically important? Give examples.

8 Can whatever can be said at all be said clearly? (T:Preface; 4.116; cf. F(GB):54–55; RPM:18,45).

9 Could there be a text-book of geometry in which, instead of theorems and proofs there were statements of theorems followed by judiciously constructed diagrams? (RFM:I.25–105; cf. Plato, *Meno* 80D–86C).

10 'The chess openings are the games of Alekhin with a few variations.' Did Alekhin by playing those games show what books on the theory of chess openings attempt to say?

11 'Now, for the poet, he nothing affirms and therefore never lieth' (Sir Philip Sydney). If we nevertheless learn from a work of fiction, is what we learn something that is shown rather than said?

9

SCEPTICISM

TEXTS:

T: 4.1121
I: 1.84, 243-315, 348-412
Z: 402-439
C: *passim*

READINGS:

1 Descartes, *Discourse on Method;* parts I and II

2 JPP: I.216-223

3 C. H. Whiteley, 'Epistemological Strategies'; *Mind* 78 (1969), 25-34

4 J. Wisdom, *Other Minds;* Oxford: Basil Blackwell, 1952

SCEPTICISM

QUESTIONS:

1 What is *methodical* doubt? (cf. Readings 1 and 4).

2 ' "What sometimes happens might always happen" ' (I:1.345). Is this true? Might, e.g. every judgment of perception or of memory be mistaken?

3 'Justification by experience comes to an end' (I:1.485).
'Doubting has an end' (I:2.v, p.180).
Is this end something indubitable that needs no justification?

4 Is it reasonable to demand that every empirical proposition should be testable? (C:109–150).

5 '. . . In order to doubt whether someone else is in pain he needs, not pain, but the *concept* "pain" ' (Z:548; cf. I:1.253–254). What would it be to have pain and lack the concept, or conversely?

6 'Not every false belief . . . is a mistake' (C:72). Give examples.

7 'Asking whether and how a proposition can be verified is only a particular way of asking "How d'you mean?" The answer is a contribution to the grammar of the proposition.' (I:1.353) Explain.

8 Does someone who rejects sense-data thereby deny the existence of sensations? (cf.I:1.486).

9 'Pity, one may say, is a form of conviction that someone else is in pain' (I:1.287). Explain the point of this remark. (cf.I:2.iv).

10 Does a result of calculation become more certain the more times I check it? (C:77; cf. C:292–299).

11 'When one hears Moore say "I *know* that that's a tree", one suddenly understands those who think that that has by no means been settled. The matter strikes one all at once as being unclear and blurred. It is as if Moore had put it in the wrong light' (C:481).
How is it put in the wrong light?

12 'It is as if "I know" did not tolerate a metaphysical emphasis' (C:482). Explain. Does this also apply to "I doubt"?

10

PRIVATE LANGUAGES

TEXTS:

BIB: 46ff.
I: 1.243–315, 348–412

READINGS:

1 Descartes, *Meditations* V

2 Kant, *Critique of Pure Reason:* Refutation of Idealism (Kemp Smith translation, 244–252)

3 JPP. I:187–196

4 Schlick, *Gesammelte Aufsätze;* The Hague: Martinus Nijhoff, 1938; Form and Content, an Introduction to Philosophical Thinking, 151–251 (especially chapter I, The Nature of Expression, 152–183)

5 R. Rhees, 'Can there be a Private Language?'
(a) in *Proceedings of the Aristotelian Society* Supp.vol.28 (1954) 77–94
(b) in *Wittgenstein: The Philosophical Investigations*, edited by George Pitcher; London: Macmillan, 1968; 267–285
(c) re-printed in R. Rhees, *Discussions of Wittgenstein;* London: Routledge and Kegan Paul, 1970; 55–70

6 N. Malcolm, 'Wittgenstein's *Philosophical Investigations'*; as 5(b), 65–103

7 P. Feyerabend, 'Wittgenstein's *Philosophical Investigations'*; ibid., 104–150

8 J. W. Cook, 'Wittgenstein on Privacy'; ibid., 286–323

9 A. Donagan, 'Wittgenstein on Sensation'; ibid., 324–351

10 A. Kenny, 'Cartesian Privacy'; ibid., 352–370

PRIVATE LANGUAGES

QUESTIONS:

1 What is the force of the 'can' in 'what can only be known to the person speaking'? (I:1.243; cf. I:1.272).

2 'Naming is so far not a move in the language-game' (I:1.49). Why not? (cf.I:1.257–258).

3 Why is the diary procedure unsuccessful? (I:1.256–265).

4 Give an example of someone thinking he understands the meaning of a word, but not really meaning anything by it (I:1.269).

5 'Looking up a table in the imagination is no more looking up a table than the image of a result of an imagined experiment is the result of an experiment' (I:1.265). Is a calculation that is imagined similarly disqualified? (cf. RFM:1.36–39, 2.55 and Reading 2).

6 'The proposition "Sensations are private" is comparable to "One plays patience by oneself"' (I:1.248). Where does the comparison lie? (cf.I:1.251).

7 Is there a distinction between having the very same sort of pain and the same individual pain? (I:1.253–254; cf.I:1.213–216, 350, 377; and Reading 8).

8 Are the words 'I am in pain' ever, for Wittgenstein, a description of a state of mind? (I:2.ix;cf.I:1.291–292).

9 Could I have an hallucination that I am in pain? (I:1.288).

10 In what circumstances does Wittgenstein think that 'A knows that' in 'A knows that p' is redundant or absurd? (I:1.246–249; cf.I:1.679).

11 What's wrong with saying that 'red' has a primary application, of which we are aware, and a secondary application to objects? (I:1.273–280; cf.I:1. 670; Z:413–436).

12 What makes an hypothesis 'a mere ornament' (I:1.270)? (cf.Z:251).

13 What is Wittgenstein's own view about the beetle in the box? (I:1.289–304; cf.Z:649 and Readings 8 and 9).

14 Is Wittgenstein a behaviourist in disguise? (I:1.305–308,311; cf.I:2.v).

11

FOLLOWING A RULE

TEXTS:

N: 49 (22.5.15: confuses dots of laziness with 'and so on'); 89-90. (cf. T:5.501
   (3) and I:1.208)
T: 5.2523 (General term of a formal series, 5.2521-5.2523)
PB: 149
BrB: 1.18-43
I: 1.85-91, 143-243
Z: 276-330
RFM: 1.2f., 8-10, 35-40, 119-126, 162f. (cf. reading from Łukasiewicz, topic 7);
   3.48-49

READINGS:

1 Kant, *Critique of Pure Reason* (Kemp Smith translation, p.177-178)

2 F(GB): 111-116

3 M. A. E. Dummett, 'Wittgenstein's Philosophy of Mathematics'
   (a) in *The Philosophical Review* 68 (1959), 324-348
   (b) in *Wittgenstein: The Philosophical Investigations*, edited by George
   Pitcher; 420-447
   (c) in *Philosophy of Mathematics: Selected Readings*, edited by Benacerraf
   and Putnam; Oxford: Basil Blackwell, 1964; 491-509

FOLLOWING A RULE

QUESTIONS:

1 ' "But *are* the steps then *not* determined by the algebraic formula?"—
The question contains a mistake.' (I:1.189). What mistake? (I:1.185–190).

2 What are the two uses of 'and so on'? (I:1.208; cf.N:49,89–90; T:5.501
(5); Z:272–278; RPM:342).

3 Could someone continue a series anyhow and still be following the rule?
(RFM:1.116; cf.I:1.143-150; BrB:1.18-43; Z:293-308).

4 'Following a rule is analogous to obeying an order' (I:1.206). Expound
the analogy (cf.I:1.458–461).

5 'It would almost be more correct to say, not that an intuition was needed
at every stage, but that a new decision was needed at every stage' (I:1.186).
Evaluate this suggestion.

6 ' "Mastery" of a technique' (I:1.150). How does this remark apply to
sudden understanding? (I:1.150–155, 179–184).

7 What light does the notion of *fitting* throw on that of *understanding*?
(I:1.182).

8 If I read aloud from a text, does seeing the text cause my utterances?
(I:1.156–164).

9 If I read aloud from a text, do I have a feeling that seeing the text causes
my utterances? (I:1.165–178).

10 Why is it explanatory to say that a process is performed 'mechanically'?
(I:1.191–197; cf. RFM:1.119–128, 3.48–49).

11 Is there a *natural* terminus to explanations? (I:1.84–87; cf. Z:309–316).

12 What is the connexion between human agreement and truth? (I:1.198–
243; RFM:1.App.2.4; Z:428–432).

12

MEANING AND USE

TEXTS:

T: 3.3, 3.326–7 (especially 4.002, 6.211)
PB: 12–15
BrB: 1.1–10
I: 1.1–36; 65–78; 549–569 (see also 'language-game', 'form of life', 'purpose' and 'point' in Index).
RFM: 1.141–152; 4.1–8; 5.7–8

READINGS:

1 Whewell and Mill on 'Types' [see Appendix 3] (to be read in conjunction with I:1.65–78)

2 R. Rhees, introduction to Wittgenstein, *The Blue and Brown Books*

3 R. Rhees, 'Wittgenstein's Builders'
    (a) in *Proceedings of the Aristotelian Society* 60 (1959–60)
    (b) re-printed in R. Rhees, *Discussions of Wittgenstein*; 71–84

MEANING AND USE

1 What does Wittgenstein mean by a language-game? (I:1.1–7).

2 'That philosophical concept of meaning has its place in a primitive idea of the way language functions' (I:1.2). What concept of meaning?

3 '. . . an over-simple conception of the script' (I:1.4). Does this judgment of Wittgenstein's represent a change from the *Tractatus*? (T:4.011–4.013).

4 '*All* tools serve to modify something' (I:1.14). What is Wittgenstein's criticism of this remark? (I:1.23–24).

5 What does Wittgenstein mean by 'use' (*Gebrauch*)? (I:1.9–17; T:3.362–3.363; I:1.549–569, 2.ii; cf.Z:691 with I:1.16, last sentence).

6 'Conceive this as a complete primitive language.' (I:1.2). Are there any difficulties in doing so?

7 '. . . if the place is already prepared' (I:1.31). What is the force of this qualification?

8 What connexion is there between Wittgenstein's stress on the relation between meaning and use and Frege's doctrine that only in the context of a proposition does a name refer?

9 'A game is a conventionalized activity designed for recreational purposes.' How would Wittgenstein seek to show that such a general definition of 'game' won't do? (cf. Appendix 3).

10 'Lying is a language-game that needs to be learned like any other' (I:1.249). Is there one consistent notion of a language game throughout the *Investigations*?

11 'The kinds of use we feel to be the "point" are connected with the role that such-and-such a use has in our whole life' (RFM:1.16). What is the connexion?

12 'Now isn't it queer that I say that the word "is" is used with two different meanings (as the copula and as the sign of equality) and should not care to say that its meaning is its use; its use, that is, as the copula and the sign of equality?' (I:1.561). Why does Wittgenstein find this queer? How radically does I:1.552–568 modify what is said in the earlier parts of the book?

13

MEANING, UNDERSTANDING, INTENDING

TEXTS:

PB: 21, 24, 31, 32

BrB: 2.7–25

I: 1.138–192, 195–242, 337(intention), 454–457, 588–595, 630–end; 2.ii, xi
    (pp.214–219)

Z: 1–33, 36–50, 159–165, 171–188, 193–197, 231–236

READINGS:

1 JPP: I.253f., 259–264, 472; II.486–492, 518–530

2 Stuart Hampshire, *Thought and Action;* London: Chatto and Windus,
    1959; chapter 2

3 G.E.M. Anscombe, *Intention;* Oxford: Basil Blackwell, 1963; sections 1–16

MEANING, UNDERSTANDING, INTENDING

QUESTIONS:

1. 'For a *large* class of cases—even if not for all—in which we employ the word "meaning", it can be defined thus: the meaning of a word is its use in the language' (I:1.43). Are there any exceptions?

2. 'The criteria which we accept for "fitting", "being able to", "understanding", are much more complicated than might appear at first sight' (I:1.182). Describe some of them, referring to the 'exercises' given earlier in this paragraph.

3. 'The game, one would like to say, has not only rules but also a *point* (*Witz*)' (I:1.564). What application does this have to an investigation of meaning? (I:1.562–568).

4. Can the intention to do something be independent of a pre-existent custom or technique? If so, in what sort of case? (I:1.205).

5. 'What is essential to intention is the picture. The picture of what is intended' (PB:21). What can be said for and against this view?

6. '. . . nothing is more wrongheaded than calling meaning (*Meinen*) a mental activity! Unless, that is, one is setting out to produce confusion' (I:1.693). What confusion is produced?

7. ' "At that word we both thought of him." . . . If God had looked into our minds he would not have been able to see there whom we were speaking of.' (I:2.xi,p.217). Explain, and explain the point of this remark.

8. 'How should we counter someone who told us that with *him*, understanding was an inner process?' (I:2.vi,p.181).

9. 'Am I to say that any one who has an intention has an experience of tending towards something?' (I:1.591; Z:33).

10. Compare and contrast the expression of an intention with a prediction (I:1.630–632; cf. Readings 2 and 3).

11. 'What is the natural expression of an intention?' (I:1.647). Is 'natural expression' the same sort of thing here as in the case of emotion?

14

THINKING

THINKING

QUESTIONS:

1 'In order to get clear about the meaning of the word "think" we watch ourselves while we think; what we observe will be what the word means.' (I:1.316; cf.1.314). What is wrong with doing this?

2 'Does a *Gedanke* consist of words?' (Russell). 'No! But of psychical constituents that have the same sort of relation to reality as words. What those constituents are I don't know' (Wittgenstein). (N:130; cf. T:5.541– 542 and Reading 2). Discuss.

3 'Thinking is an incorporeal process' (I:1.339). In what circumstances would this be a useful piece of information? (cf. Z:123–127).

4 'Misleading parallel: the expression of pain is a cry—the expression of thought, a proposition' (I:1.317). In what way misleading? (cf.JPP: I.477–479, footnote).

5 'The criteria for the truth of the confession that I thought such-and-such are not the criteria for a true description of a process' (I:2.xi,p.222). Expound this distinction.

6 Thinking is 'what distinguishes speech with thought from talking without thinking' (I:1.330). Will this do?

7 '... we cannot separate his "thinking" from his activity' (Z:101). Why not?

8 'If I say I have thought—need I always be right?—What *kind* of mistake is there room for here?' (I:1.328).

9 Could Mr Ballard's memory be trusted? (I:1.342; cf. Z:108–109; JPP:I.266ff.).

10 'This shews you how different the grammar of the verb "to mean" (*meinen*) is from that of "to think"' (I:1.693). Expound the difference.

11 Is the communication of a thought from one person to another like sending a message by teleprinter? (I:2.xi,p.222; cf. JPP:I.219–220).

12 'The chair is thinking to itself:. . .' (I:1.361). Construct a story containing this sentence (you can fill in the dots as you please). (cf. Z:127–131).

13 What would show *why* a man thinks? (I:1.468; cf. 1.466–470).

15

FEELINGS

QUESTIONS:

1   Why would Wittgenstein object to the use of a general term such as Descartes' *'cogitatio'* (cf. Readings 1 and 2). Are his objections justifiable?

2   What does Wittgenstein mean by 'genuine duration', and why does he attach importance to the notion? (Z:472, 478, 488; cf. I:1.p.59,notes).

3   ' "Joy" designates nothing at all. Neither any inward nor any outward thing' (Z:487). Why should Wittgenstein say this?

4   'Love is not a feeling. Love is put to the test, pain not' (Z:504). Is this true?

5   'How much analogy is there between delight and what we call e.g. "sensation"? The connecting link between them would be pain' (Z:484–485). How would pain form a connexion?

6   'But if one wanted to find an analogy to the place of pain, it would of course not be the mind (as, of course, the place of bodily pain is not the body) but the *object* of regret' (Z:511). How like is the place of pain to the object of regret?

7   'If anyone asks whether pleasure is a sensation, he probably does not distinguish between reason and cause' (Z:507). How does this show the difference?

8   Can we distinguish between feeling a sensation and feeling an emotion? (Z:486–527).

9   'Belief . . . is a sort of feeling more allied to the emotions than to anything else' (JPP:II.283). Is it? (cf. I:1.225ff., 607; Z:513).

10   'The if-feeling is not a feeling which accompanies the word "if" ' (I:2.vi,p.182; cf. I:2.vi; Z:188; JPP:I.245–246,252; Reading 3).

16

FULFILMENT
of possibility, wish, expectation, etc.

TEXTS:

PB: 11, 16, 21–35
BlB: 20 ff.
I: 1.193–194, 437–445, 452–453, 458–461, 465 (cf. T:4.023)
Z: 53–63, 68–70, 284–290
Lectures and Conversations on Aesthetics, Psychology and Religious Belief;
    edited by Cyril Barrett from notes taken by Yorick Smithies, Rush Rhees
    and James Taylor; Oxford: Basil Blackwell, 1966; Conversations on
    Freud, 41–52 (for question 9).

READINGS:

1   JPP: II.251 (expectation), 320–321, I: 249–256

2   Freud, *The Interpretation of Dreams;* London: Allen and Unwin, 1937 (for
    question 9)

3   Russell, *The Analysis of Mind;* London: Allen and Unwin, 1921; lecture III

FULFILMENT
of possibility, wish, expectation, etc.

QUESTIONS:

1 'Could we imagine a language in which expecting p was not described by means of p? Isn't that just as impossible as a language in which $\sim p$ would be expressed without using p?' (PB:30).

2 'To what extent does an order anticipate its execution?' (I:1.461).

3 'Expecting is connected with looking for' (PB:28). Expand the connexion. (cf. I:1.685).

4 'Another mental process which belongs to this group, and which is connected with all these things, is *intention*' (PB:31). Compare the execution of an intention or of an order with the fulfilment of a wish or of an expectation.

5 Distinguish:
(a) the satisfaction of an instinct (e.g. hunger) from the satisfaction of an expectation or wish;
(b) the satisfaction of an expectation from the satisfaction of a wish (cf. PB:21–22; JPP:II.320–321).

6 'It is not the person expected that is the fulfilment, but rather his coming' (Z:58). What point is Wittgenstein making?

7 'A proposition, and hence in another sense a thought, can be the "expression" of belief, hope, expectation, etc. But believing is not thinking. (A grammatical remark). The concepts of believing, expecting, hoping are less distantly related to one another than they are to the concept of thinking' (I:1.574). Is Wittgenstein justified in putting belief with expectation, etc.? (I:1.574–577; cf. Z:71–86).

8 'In order to understand the grammar of these states it is necessary to ask: "What counts as a criterion for anyone's being in such a state?"' (I:1.572). How do answers to this question elucidate the grammar of states?

9 Does it make sense to say that a dream is a wish-fulfilment? (cf. Reading 2).

17

THE MYSTICAL AND THE ETHICAL

TEXTS:

N: 72 (11.6.16)–86, 91(10.1.17)

T: 5.6–5.641, 6.37–7

'Wittgenstein's Lecture on Ethics'; *The Philosophical Review* 74 (1965), 3–26
(particularly for question 4)

Lectures and Conversations on Aesthetics, Psychology and Religious Belief;
53–59

READINGS:

1 Schopenhauer, *The World as Will and Idea*:
a I.133–137, 167–168 ('egoism' = 'solipsism')
b I.360–362, 364–366 (living in the present)
c I.452–454 (ethical reward and punishment)
d I.515–517 (suicide)
e I.529–532 (world of the happy and the unhappy)
f I.532; III.427 ('the rest is silence')
g II.373 ff. ('*that* the world is . . .')

2 Tolstoy, 'How much Land does a Man need?' in *Twenty-Three Tales;*
London: Oxford University Press, 1906 (The World's Classics, 72);
207–226

3 Tolstoy, 'The Death of Ivan Ilych'; in *Ivan Ilych and Hadji Murad;*
London: Oxford University Press (The World's Classics, 432)

4 Frege, 'The Thought' (reference under Topic 4, Reading 2)

5 Bradley, *Essays on Truth and Reality;* Oxford: at the Clarendon Press, 1914;
pp.468–469

6 AT:170–171

7 Engelmann, *Letters from Ludwig Wittgenstein;* Oxford: Basil Blackwell,
1967

8 McGuinness, 'The Mysticism of the Tractatus': *The Philosophical
Review* 75 (1966), 305–328

THE MYSTICAL AND THE ETHICAL

QUESTIONS:

1 What does Wittgenstein mean by 'mystical'? (T:6.44–6.45, 6.522; cf. Reading 8)

2 'We feel that even if *all possible* scientific questions be answered, the problems of life have still not been touched at all. Of course, there is then no question left and just this is the answer' (T:6.52). Expound.

3 '. . . what the solipsist *means* (*meint*) is quite correct; only it cannot be said, but shows itself'. Expound. (cf. N:80, 82, 85; Readings 1a and 4).

4 'It is clear that ethics cannot be put into words' (T:6.421). Why not? (cf. N:79).

5 'He lives eternally who lives in the present.' Is there such a thing as *not* living in the present? (N:75; Schopenhauer, I.360–362; T:6.4311; Matthew 6:25–34).

6 'The world of the happy man is a different one from that of the unhappy one' (T:6.43). In what way different? (cf. N:78–79).

7 'To believe in God means to see that life has a meaning' (N:74). Discuss.

8 'The act of the will is not the cause of the action but is the action itself' (N:87; cf. I:1.611–624). Did Wittgenstein's view about willing undergo a change between the *Notebooks* and the *Investigations*?

9 'The world is independent of my will' (T:6.373). Is this consistent with Wittgenstein's view in the *Notebooks* (N:86,88)?

10 '. . . the suicide is like a sick man who, after a painful operation which would entirely cure him has been begun, will not allow it to be completed, but prefers to retain his disease' (Schopenhauer I.516). Is this an apt comparison? (cf. N:91).

THE NATURE OF PHILOSOPHY

TEXTS:

N: 44, 93
T: Author's Preface; 4.003–4.0031, 4.111–4.121, 6.53–6.54
PB: Preface; 1–9, 54
I: Preface, 1.89–90, 109–133, 144, 192–196, 216, 251–255, 309, 314, 436, 464, 593, 599, 2.xiv
RFM: 1, Appendix 1.4
Z: 314, 323, 328, 382, 447–467
C: 318–319

READINGS:

1 Kant, *Critique of Pure Reason*, Preface to Second Edition (Kemp Smith translation, 17–37)
2 Russell, *Our Knowledge of the External World;* London: Allen and Unwin, 1922; lecture I, Current Tendencies, and lecture II, Logic as the Essence of Philosophy; 13–69 (for questions 8 and 9)
3 G. Ryle, 'Systematically Misleading Expressions'
   (a) in *Proceedings of the Aristotelian Society* 32 (1931–32), 139–170
   (b) re-printed in *Logic and Language* (first series) edited by Anthony Flew; Oxford: Basil Blackwell, 1955; 11–36
4 Austin, 'Are There A Priori Concepts?'
   (a) in *Proceedings of the Aristotelian Society*, Supplementary Volume 18 (1939), 83–105
   (b) re-printed in J. L. Austin, *Philosophical Papers;* Oxford: at the Clarendon Press, 1961; 1–22
5 Erik Stenius, *Wittgenstein's Tractatus: A Critical Exposition of its Main Lines of Thought;* Oxford: Basil Blackwell, 1960; chapter XI
6 J. Wisdom, 'The Metamorphosis of Metaphysics' (for question 10)
   (a) in *Proceedings of the British Academy* 47 (1961), 37–59
   (b) re-printed in John Wisdom, *Paradox and Discovery;* Oxford: Basil Blackwell, 1965; 57–81
7 S. Cavell, 'The Availability of Wittgenstein's Later Philosophy'
   (a) in *The Philosophical Review* 71 (1962), 67–93
   (b) re-printed in *Wittgenstein: The Philosophical Investigations*, edited by George Pitcher; 151–185
   (c) re-printed in S. Cavell, *Must we Mean what we Say?* New York: Charles Scribner's Sons, 1969; 44–72

THE NATURE OF PHILOSOPHY

QUESTIONS:

1 'It was Russell who performed the service of showing that the apparent logical form of a proposition need not be its real one' (T:4.0031). Give examples of propositions which could mislead one as to their form (cf.I:1.664).

2 Does Wittgenstein use the term 'grammar' metaphorically? (I:1.251–252).

3 'My aim is: to teach you to pass from a piece of disguised nonsense to something that is patent nonsense' (I:1.464; cf. I:1.350 for an example). Give further examples.

4 'We feel as if we had to *penetrate* phenomena: our investigation, however, is directed not towards phenomena, but . . . towards the "*possibilities*" of phenomena' (I:1.90). Compare this with Kant's conception of metaphysics.

5 'If one tried to advance *theses* in philosophy, it would never be possible to debate them, because everyone would agree to them' (I:1.128). Elucidate.

6 'The philosopher's treatment of a question is like the treatment of an illness' (I:1.255; cf. RFM:1. App.2.4). Explain.

7 'In philosophizing we may not *terminate* a disease of thought. It must run its natural course, and *slow* cure is all important. (That is why mathematicians are such bad philosophers)' (Z:382). What reason could be given for this?

8 'A main cause of philosophical disease—a one-sided diet: one nourishes one's thinking with only one kind of example' (I:1.593; cf. C:31). Cite cases. (cf. Reading 2).

9 'It is one of the chief skills of the philosopher not to occupy himself with questions which do not concern him' (N:44; cf. I:1.124–126). To what extent is knowledge of a particular subject (mathematics, physics, psychology, theology) irrelevant to the philosophy of that subject? (cf. Reading 2).

10 'One might say that the subject we are dealing with is one of the heirs of the subject which used to be called "philosophy"' (BlB:28; cf. motto to I from Nestroy). Is the contrast between what Wittgenstein is doing and what previous philosophers were doing as great as he thought? (cf. BlB:62; cf. Reading 6).

Further Topics
suitable for additional work

1 Grammar

2 Logical space (grammar and geometry)

3 Negation

4 Generality

5 Infinity

6 The notion of a foundation for arithmetic

7 Identity

8 The assertion sign

9 Inference

10 Probability

11 Causality

12 Propositions as truth-functions of elementary propositions

13 The general form of proposition

14 Definiteness of sense

15 Family resemblance

16 Perspicuous representation

17 'Seeing as'

18 Images (calculating in the head)

19 Emotions

20 The will

21 Way of life

PASSAGES PARALLEL TO WITTGENSTEIN'S *TRACTATUS* IN RUSSELL'S *THE PRINCIPLES OF MATHEMATICS*

Russell para:	Wittgenstein
1	6.1231
7	4.126–4.1272, 5.5351–5.5352, 6.022
14	5.5351
16	5.42 (interdefinability of ⊃' and other signs)
	5.5351, 5.47–5.472 (definition of 'proposition')
18 (axiom (4))	5.452
24	6.031
28, end	5.5357
30, beginning	5.461, 5.42
38	4.442, 5.132, 5.452, 6.1264
41	5.5351
42	(5.501, 5.502), 5.52, 5.521
44, end	6.1231
46, beginning	4.002, 4.0312, 5.5563
47	4.1272, 5.53–5.5351
52	4.063, end; 4.0641
53	4.1274
78	3.333
81	3.315, 5.52–5.523
83	5.5351
85	3.333
86 (also 93)	3.315–3.317
95	4.0312, 4.441, 5.5301, 5.4
96	3.333
99	3.1432
100, beginning	4.1272
101	3.333
109	6.02–6.031
118	4.1273
135–136	3.14–3.144
404	6.36111
440	6.3751
442	2.024–2.0272, 5.541–5.5421
443	2.024–2.0272
449	5.135–5.1361, 6.37–6.372, 6.375
453–454	6.341–6.342
462	6.3–6.34, 6.343–6.3432
475	3.144, 3.221, 3.3
477–479	4.442, 4.063–4.0641
480	5.02, 5.521–5.523
483	3.315–3.317
495	4.1273

Appendix 2

PASSAGES PARALLEL TO WITTGENSTEIN'S *PHILOSOPHICAL INVESTIGATIONS* AND *ZETTEL* IN JAMES'S *THE PRINCIPLES OF PSYCHOLOGY*

James		Wittgenstein
Vol. I:		
183–185	Psychology as a natural science	I:1.571; 2.xiv (232)
185–186	Thought and feeling assimilated	I:1.317, 501; Z:84
191, 241, 244, 246, 251–256	Thought is elusive and indescribable in language	I:1.273–9, 308, 435f., 610
219ff.	Difficulties of getting things across to others	I:1.283, 363, 431–3; Z:256
225–7, 321–342	Ownership of experiences, personal identity	I:1.253, 398, 403–411
245–7, 252	Feelings of *if*, *but*, etc.	I:2.vi (181–183), xi (214); Z:188
249–255	Intention, trying, feelings of tendency	I:1.139, 334–337, 633–648, 657–660; 2.xi (218–220); Z:33, 38, 44–48
252, 259–265, 275–283	Sense of familiarity, 'fringe' experiences	I:1.530–535, 595–6, 598, 600–606, 609; 2.vi (181, 183); Z:155–190
252–4, 278–283	Producing and understanding sentences	I:1.498–500, 511–513, 525, 652; 2.ii (175–176), vi (181–183); Z:38, 153–4, 176, 188, 191, 247–248
266–268	Thought without language (the Ballard case)	I:1.342; Z:109
278–283	'Meanings' as mental accompaniments	I:1.329–332, 507–510; 2.ii (175–176); Z:155–185
297–305	The Self of selves	I:1.398, 403–411
623–624(n)	Judging what time it is	I:1.607–608
648–652	Memory	I:1.305–306; 2.xiii (231); Z:650–668
Vol. II		
37–43	Sensations 'projected' outside body	I:1.626
44–75	Imagination and sense	I:1.385–388, 443; Z:621–646
134–144	'Extensity' of sensations	Z:479–483
191–197, 488–494	Sensations of position and motion	I:2.viii (185–186); Z:472, 479–483
283–4, 307–11	Belief-feelings	I:1.589–590; 2.xi(225); Z:513
458–462	Emotions and bodily feelings	I:2.ix (187); Z:486, 492, 495–499, 512
559–565	Will, attention, effort	I:1.611–632; Z:576–601

Appendix 3

WHEWELL AND MILL ON TYPES [see topic 12]

W. Whewell, *History of Scientific Ideas*, II, 120–122

Natural groups are given by Type, not by Definition. And this consideration accounts for that indefiniteness and indecision which we frequently find in the descriptions of such groups, and which must appear so strange and inconsistent to any one who does not suppose these descriptions to assume any deeper ground of connexion than an arbitrary choice of the botanist. Thus in the family of the rose-tree, we are told that the *ovules* are *very rarely* erect, the *stigmata usually* simple. Of what use, it might be asked, can such loose accounts be? To which the answer is, that they are not inserted in order to distinguish the species, but in order to describe the family, and the total relations of the ovules and the stigmata of the family are better known by this general statement. A similar observation may be made with regard to the Anomalies of each group, which occur so commonly, that Mr Lindley, in his *Introduction to the Natural System of Botany*, makes the 'Anomalies' an article in each family. Thus, part of the character of the Rosaceae is, that they have alternate *stipulate* leaves, and that the *albumen* is *obliterated*: but yet in *Lowea*, one of the genera of this family, the stipulae are *absent*; and the albumen is *present* in another, *Neillia*. This implies, as we have already seen, that the artificial character (or *diagnosis*, as Mr Lindley calls it) is imperfect. It is, though very nearly, yet not exactly, commensurate with the natural group: and hence in certain cases this character is made to yield to the general weight of natural affinities.

These views,—of classes determined by characters which cannot be expressed in words,—of propositions which state, not what happens in all cases, but only usually,— of particulars which are included in a class, though they transgress the definition of it, may probably surprise the reader. They are so contrary to many of the received opinions respecting the use of definitions, and the nature of scientific propositions, that they will probably appear to many persons highly illogical and unphilosophical. But a disposition to such a judgment arises in a great measure from this, that the mathematical and mathematico-physical sciences have, in a great degree, determined men's views of the general nature and form of scientific truth; while Natural History has not yet had time or opportunity to exert its due influence upon the current habits of philosophizing. The apparent indefiniteness and inconsistency of the classifications and definitions of Natural History belongs, in a far higher degree, to all other except mathematical speculations; and the modes in which approximations to exact distinctions and general truths have been made in Natural History, may be worthy of our attention, even for the light they throw upon the best modes of pursuing truth of all kinds.

Though in a Natural group of objects a definition can no longer be of any use as a regulative principle, classes are not therefore left quite loose, without any certain standard or guide. The class is steadily fixed, though not precisely limited; it is given, though not circumscribed; it is determined, not by a boundary line without, but by a

49

central point within; not by what it strictly excludes, but by what it eminently includes; by an example, not by a precept; in short, instead of a Definition we have a Type for our director.

A Type is an example of any class, for instance a species of a genus, which is considered as eminently possessing the character of the class. All the species which have a greater affinity with this type-species than with any others, form the genus, and are arranged about it, deviating from it in various directions and different degrees. Thus a genus may consist of several species which approach very near the type, and of which the claim to a place with it is obvious; while there may be other species which straggle further from this central knot, and which yet are clearly more connected with it than with any other. And even if there should be some species of which the place is dubious, and which appear to be equally bound to two generic types, it is easily seen that this would not destroy the reality of the generic groups, any more than the scattered trees of the intervening plain prevent our speaking intelligibly of the distinct forests of two separate hills.

The type-species of every genus, the type-genus of every family, is, then, one which possesses all the characters and properties of the genus in a marked and prominent manner. The type of the Rose family has alternate stipulate leaves, wants the albumen, has the ovules not erect, has the stigmata simple, and besides these features, which distinguish it from the exceptions or varieties of its class, it has the features which make it prominent in its class. It is one of those which possess clearly several leading attributes; and thus, though we cannot say of any one genus that it *must* be the type of the family, or of any one species that it *must* be the type of the genus, we are still not wholly to seek; the type must be connected by many affinities with most of the others of its group; it must be near the centre of the crowd, and not one of the stragglers.

J. S. Mill, *A System of Logic;* Longmans 1865, II. 276–277

Though the groups are suggested by types, I cannot think that a group when formed is determined by the type; that in deciding whether a species belongs to the group, a reference is made to the type, and not to the characters; that the characters 'cannot be expressed in words'. This assertion is inconsistent with Dr Whewell's own statement of the fundamental principle of classification, namely, that 'general assertions shall be possible'. If the class did not possess any characters in common, what general assertions would be possible respecting it? Except that they all resemble each other more than they resemble anything else, nothing whatever could be predicated of the class.

The truth is, on the contrary, that every genus or family is framed with distinct reference to certain characters, and is composed, first and principally, of species which agree in possessing all those characters. To these are added, as a sort of appendix, such other species, general in small number, as possess *nearly* all the properties selected; wanting some of them one property, some another, and which, while they agree with the rest *almost* as much as these agree with one another, do not resemble in an equal degree any other group. Our conception of the class continues to be grounded on the characters; and the class might be defined, those things which *either* possess that set of characters, *or* resemble the things that do so, more than they resemble anything else.

And this resemblance itself is not, like resemblance between simple sensations, an ultimate fact, unsusceptible of analysis. Even the inferior degree of resemblance is created by the possession of common characters. Whatever resembles the genus Rose more than it resembles any other genus, does so because it possesses a greater number of the characters of that genus, than of the characters of any other genus. Nor can there be the smallest difficulty in representing, by an enumeration of characters, the nature and degree of the resemblance which is strictly sufficient to include any object in the class. There are always some properties common to all things which are included. Others there often are, to which some things, which are nevertheless included, are exceptions. But the objects which are exceptions to one character are not exceptions to another: the resemblance which fails in some particulars must be made up for in others. The class, therefore, is constituted by the possession of *all* the characters which are universal, and *most* of those which admit of exceptions. If a plant had the ovules erect, the stigmata divided, possessed the albumen, and was without stipules, it probably would not be classed among the Rosaceae. But it may want any one, or more than one of these characters, and not be excluded. The ends of a scientific classification are better answered by including it. Since it agrees so nearly, in its known properties, with the sum of the characters of the class, it is likely to resemble that class more than any other in those of its properties which are still undiscovered.

Not only, therefore, are natural groups, no less than any artificial classes, determined by characters; they are constituted in contemplation of, and by reason of, characters. But it is in contemplation not of those characters only which are rigorously common to all the objects included in the group, but of the entire body of characters, all of which are found in most of those objects, and most of them in all. And hence our conception of the class, the image in our minds which is representative of it, is that of a specimen complete in all the characters; most naturally a specimen which, by possessing them all in the greatest degree in which they are ever found, is the best fitted to exhibit clearly, and in a marked manner, what they are. It is by a mental reference to this standard, not instead of, but in illustration of, the definition of the class, that we usually and advantageously determine whether any individual or species belongs to the class or not. And this, as it seems to me, is the amount of truth contained in the doctrine of Types.